AF647067

First published in India in 2022 by HarperCollins Children's Books
An imprint of HarperCollins *Publishers*
Building No. 10, Tower A, 4th Floor, DLF Cyber City, Phase II, Gurugram 122002
www.harpercollins.co.in

2 4 6 8 10 9 7 5 3 1

Text © Shalini Satish & Raam Baranidharan 2022
Illustrations © HarperCollins *Publishers* India 2022

P-ISBN: 978-935-4895-83-8
E-ISBN: 978-935-4896-18-7

Shalini Satish & Raam Baranidharan assert the moral right
to be identified as the authors of this work.

The views and opinions expressed in this book are the authors' own and the
facts are as reported by them, and the publishers are not in any way liable for the same.

All rights reserved. No part of this publication may be reproduced,
stored in a retrieval system, or transmitted, in any form or by any means, electronic, mechanical,
photocopying, recording or otherwise, without the prior permission of the publishers.

Cover illustration: Nishi Banka
Cover design: Nishi Banka

Typeset in Gotham Rounded 14pt/ 20

Printed and bound at Nutech Print Services - India

HarperCollinsIn

The Little Handbook of Cool Technology

Shalini Satish & Raam Baranidharan

Illustrated by Nishi Banka

HarperCollins*Children'sBooks*

Foreword

The human body and brain are about the same as they were 10,000 years ago at the dawn of civilization. Despite climate change and other serious issues, the surface of the Earth hasn't changed so dramatically either. However, the world into which young people are now born is radically different from what it was even 50 years ago when I started kindergarten. The core reason for this is, of course, technology.

Driven by science, mathematics and broad-minded creative thinking, technology has become in many ways the dominant factor in modern human life. The way we educate our children, however, has in some ways not kept up. Reading, arithmetic and history are as important as they ever were, yet it's now equally important for children to wrap their minds and hearts around the newly emerging computing and communication technologies that form such a key part of our world.

As a father of five kids, currently ranging in age from thirty-one years to six months, I've personally seen what a challenge it can be to break down the essentials of modern technology into clearly explained, entertainingly presented, bite-sized portions that are suitable for young minds to understand. So, I was quite excited when I saw this little book which meets this challenge so fantastically.

Of course, no single book can tell the full story of modern technology. There is so much going on in today's tech world that no single person can understand it all. The story changes every year with new inventions and discoveries. What is important is that young people grow up with minds that are actively curious and imaginative regarding the advanced technologies that are becoming mainstream and an integral part of our lives.

The technology of tomorrow is waiting to be created by you, dear readers! Go to it!

Ben Goertzel
Cross-disciplinary entrepreneur, scientist,
mathematician, engineer, writer, speaker
www.goertzel.org

Technology has brought the world closer and changed lives significantly. It has opened doors to the unknown and unexplored. Given how technology has woven itself into almost every aspect of life, it is important to understand and use it in an effective and responsible manner.

The Little Handbook of Cool Technology presents a conversation between young learners, Alia and Copa, about different aspects of everyday technology.

ALIA

Alia is a young girl who loves reading books and the outdoors. She is fascinated by technology and stays abreast of new developments.

COPA

Copa is a playful and inquisitive boy. He enjoys hanging out with Alia and learning new things from her.

Copa always has a bagful of questions and Alia answers them patiently. Together this duo takes you along on their fun-filled journey of exploring technology.

STYLE

This book delivers content to readers in bite-sized portions. Each spread is a logical breakout. The first occurrence of a word that introduces a concept is highlighted in colour.

TRIVIA

Blackboards sprinkled across the book contain fascinating trivia. We encourage further reading about the trivia.

ACTIVITIES

Every chapter contains activities to leave the readers with prompts for further exploration.

✏ indicates a writing activity.

🖥 indicates a typing activity.

TIPS FOR PARENTS

In the world of technology, change is the only constant. While children use gadgets effortlessly, do they understand how the gadgets work? With this book, we aim to lower the entry barrier for understanding technology and set the readers on a path of curiosity, exploration and self-learning.

"It's a timely reading tool, given the increased digital exposure and technology usage kids have in their lives today. It is important that they embrace technology with an understanding of its nuances and perils."

Reshma Krishnamurthy
Founder, Mums and Stories

"After spending a lifetime in classrooms, yearning for study material that is current, useful and on-point, I finally find just that in this book!"

Jyoti Thyagarajan
Educationalist, Founder Trustee of Meghshala Trust and Founder Director and Chief Design Officer of Ontum Education Pvt Ltd.

"Full of fascinating facts (internet cables are laid on the ocean floor by special ships with a sea plough), fun exercises and funky graphics, *The Little Handbook of Cool Technology* spells out all the mechanics of everyday technology in accessible, bite-sized bits. A breezy read for children and adults alike."

Mini Anthikad Chhibber
Deputy Editor, *The Hindu*

"This cool little handbook is an easy to read, well-illustrated guide which helps to understand and demystify everyday terms which are used in internet technology. It could be useful not just to kids, but even to adults who are unfamiliar with the net."

Gita Aravamudan
Author and Journalist

Contents

IP
www

Internet

A TREASURE TROVE OF DATA

We can spot a shooting star tonight! Let us go to the terrace and see it.

How do you know about the shooting star?

I read about it in an article on the **internet**.

What is the internet?

The internet is a network of computers across the world. A **computer** connected to the internet can access information from other computers that are also connected to the internet. When you enter the name of a website in the address bar of a **browser**, it connects to the computer hosting the website via the internet and displays the website you are looking for. A browser is a **computer program** that helps access and view websites.

The internet is a network of computers across the world.

How does our computer know where other computers are located?

Each computer has an address called an **IP address**. IP stands for **Internet Protocol**. Similar to how a residential address identifies our house uniquely, an IP address identifies each computer or device on the internet uniquely. The **router** uses the IP address to identify devices on the internet.

What is a router?

A router is like a post office that routes and delivers mail (data) to different locations (devices) and ensures that the mail reaches the correct address. The router ensures that each device, such as a smartphone, laptop or desktop within a network managed by it, has a unique number, i.e., a unique IP address so that the data reaches the right device.

The router in our house manages data flow across all our devices. The smartphone and the laptop are both connected to the internet but when we visit a website from the laptop, the website opens only on the laptop and not on the smartphone. This is because the router knows that the request for opening the website originated from the laptop.

Coming back to how computers share information. Computers send and receive data via wired and wireless mediums. We rely almost entirely on wired mediums or cables for internet traffic because they are faster and less expensive than wireless mediums, such as satellites. Most cables are laid on the ocean bed with the help of ships.

Tell me more about these cable-laying ships ...

Special cable-laying ships dig the ocean bed with an instrument called a **sea plough**. They lay cables that are used to transmit data that powers the internet. This is similar to the way farmers plough the land to sow seeds. There is a huge cable network under the ocean bed. It is like a metro rail network with stations and junctions.

The SEA-ME-WE 3 submarine cable network is close to 39,000 km in length connecting 33 countries across four continents.

These cables must be very long ...

Yes, these cables are very long and stretch across continents!

Currently, Antarctica is the only continent not wired to the internet via submarine cables.

Special devices called **repeaters** are fixed at regular intervals to the cables to amplify the signal and avoid signal loss.

What if fish and other aquatic animals bite the cables?

Sharks and other animals like to chew on submarine cables, but that is not really a problem. The cables are covered with extra strong material such as polyethylene (a hard plastic) and in some cases Kevlar that can withstand a lot of pressure. Kevlar is a strong, synthetic fibre.

There is no cable connected to our laptop. How does the laptop connect to the internet?

Our laptop connects to the router using radio waves. **Wi-Fi** is the name of a wireless networking technology that uses radio waves to provide wireless network connections. The router has a wired connection to the internet.

At times, videos I watch online get stuck. Why does that happen?

The speed with which data moves depends on the speed of the internet connection. **Buffering** is the process in which a video player downloads data before it starts playing, making it appear like the video is stuck. A slow internet connection means that the video is downloaded slowly and hence the player has to buffer for longer. Just as a vehicle's speed is measured in kilometres per hour, data flow is measured in **megabits per second (Mbps)**.

Is there a scale like a weighing scale to measure data flow?

Similar to how the weight of fruits and vegetables is measured in grams and kilograms, the size of data is measured in bytes and transfer speed is measured in megabits/second. A single letter of the alphabet like ‘x’ or ‘a’ measures one byte or eight bits.

Here is the scale for measuring data in the decimal system.

Unit of Measure	Symbol	Value in Bytes (Numbers)	Value in Bytes (Words)
Byte	B	1	one
Kilobyte	KB	1,000	one thousand
Megabyte	MB	1,000,000	one million
Gigabyte	GB	1,000,000,000	one billion
Terabyte	TB	1,000,000,000,000	one trillion
Petabyte	PB	1,000,000,000,000,000	one quadrillion

Those are really big numbers!

As technology has advanced, the ability to store data has increased and we can now transfer large amounts of data easily.

The complete rendering of the movie 'Avatar' requires 1 petabyte of storage which is equivalent to a 32-year-long MP3 file!

You have mentioned 'website' quite a few times. What is a website?

A **website** is a collection of content organized in the form of interconnected web pages. All publicly accessible **websites** form the **world wide web**, commonly abbreviated as www. Websites start with www which indicates that it is a part of the world wide web. Each website has a unique address called a **web address**.

There must be so many websites with a lot of content! How do we find what we are looking for?

We use a **search engine** to find the content we are looking for. Google Search, DuckDuckGo and Bing are popular search engines.

This information about how the internet works is just the tip of the iceberg! We will learn more as we go along this fun and exploratory journey.

Evolution of Internet in India

1986

ERNET, the first form of the internet, is made available to educational institutions.

1995

VSNL introduces the internet to the public in six cities via dial-up connections.

1996

The first cyber cafe opens in Mumbai.

1998

Online banking starts.

1999

The railway reservation system is linked nationwide.

2000

Cable internet starts and the Information Technology Act comes into effect.

2017

There are more active Facebook users in India than in the United States.

2019

India has more than 500 million internet users.

1 Can you find these words about the internet in the grid below?

- COMPUTER
- WORLD WIDE WEB
- MEGABIT
- SEA PLOUGH
- INTERNET
- WEBSITE
- REPEATER
- ROUTER
- PROTOCOL
- BROWSER

P	R	B	M	E	G	A	B	I	T	R	C	S
R	V	I	N	T	E	R	N	E	T	E	B	E
O	B	R	O	W	S	E	R	E	W	D	Y	A
T	N	C	L	C	A	W	N	S	O	N	T	P
O	S	O	R	E	W	E	B	S	I	T	E	L
C	B	M	R	O	S	E	G	N	U	O	F	O
O	P	P	S	E	U	S	I	L	T	E	R	U
L	O	U	L	E	P	T	P	Q	U	E	V	G
S	Z	T	P	E	R	E	E	N	E	C	L	H
Z	L	E	L	M	P	Q	U	R	G	E	B	U
W	O	R	L	D	W	I	D	E	W	E	B	R
O	W	Q	U	W	E	S	J	B	U	F	G	G
S	B	R	E	P	E	A	T	E	R	E	Y	E

2 Find the speed of your internet connection.

1. Open the browser on your computer.
2. Type 'speed test' in the search bar of the browser.
3. Go to a website that supports speed tests.
4. Write down the upload and download speed of your internet connection.

Upload speed: ____________________

Download speed: ____________________

3 Find your IP address.

1. Open the browser on your computer.
2. Type 'My IP address' in the search bar of the browser.
3. Write down the IP address of your computer.

IP address: ____________________

Does it change every day? ____________________

How many digits does the IP address have? ____________________

4 Know your browser.

____

Name of the browser on your computer

____

Name of the company that developed the browser

5 View the internet highways.

1. Open the browser on your computer.
2. Type 'submarine cable map' in the search bar of the browser.
3. See the various undersea cables around the world.

6 List your favourite websites.

Website	Website Address
Radish Tales	www.radishtales.com

7 Pick your favourite colour pencil and draw the Wi-Fi signal.

Search Engine

FINDING A NEEDLE IN A HAYSTACK

The internet is so vast! How do we find what we are looking for on the internet?

As you know by now, millions of computers across the world are connected to the internet. The collective 'knowledge' on the internet is much more than the knowledge any person can have. We need an easy way to find the information we are looking for. This is where **search engines** such as Google Search, Bing and DuckDuckGo help. A search engine 'answers' the question by finding information on the internet. This is like finding a needle in a haystack but the search engine makes it look easy.

How is information stored on the internet?

Information on the internet is organized as **websites**. A website is a collection of content organized in the form of interconnected web pages under one **web address**.

Websites are connected by **hyperlinks**. A hyperlink is a reference to a website that a user can follow by clicking on it. It is a coded word or image that when clicked takes the user to another website.

How does a search engine work?

A search engine has a program called **spider** that collects information from websites. The spider scans websites provided to it by website creators and websites it visited in previous scans. The spider visits each website and then follows every hyperlink that it finds on the website and navigates to related websites to collect information. This process of navigating the entire web of interconnected websites is called **crawling**.

Spiders, webs and crawling. This is like a world of creepy-crawlies! What does the spider do with the information that it collects from each website?

The spider stores the information it collects from each website in an **index**. The index makes it easy to find information. The spider updates the index continuously.

A search engine has a program called **spider** that collects information from websites.

What is an index?

In books, an index is a list of words and page numbers where the respective words occur. It helps us find pages of the book through keywords. Similarly, a search engine's index helps the search engine find matches for a given search phrase.

How does a search engine use the index?

A search engine's index has words and a list of websites that contain the words.

When you search for a word or phrase, the search engine uses the index to find the information in a 3-step process:

1. Split the search phrase into words.
2. Search the index for each word in the search phrase.
3. Retrieve all websites that contain the words in the search phrase.

For example, if the search phrase is ‘flying bats’, the search engine would split the phrase into two words, ‘flying’ and ‘bats’. The search engine will then search the index and retrieve websites that contain these words.

There are so many websites where a search phrase occurs. How does a search engine decide the order of display of the search results?

The words in a search phrase can appear on many websites and the search can produce a large number of results. Search engines use a combination of several factors and the context of the search to determine the most relevant results.

What is the context of a search?

Let us take an example to understand the 'context of a search'. When you search for 'wooden bat', the search engine knows that you are searching for a sports bat. When you search for 'flying bat', it knows that you are searching for the animal. Just as numbers can be ordered in ascending or descending order, search results can be ordered by **relevance**.

PageRank is Google's search algorithm. The rank of a web page is determined by the number of hyperlinks to it. The more the number of hyperlinks to a page, the higher its rank.

Does the index have information from all the computers in the world?

No, it does not have all the information from all computers in the world. Websites can be set up so that certain web pages are not crawled using special instructions that the spider can understand. Photographs or information on your personal computer cannot be discovered by a search engine.

The name PageRank is not based on the term 'web page' but comes from the creator of the algorithm – Larry Page. Larry Page and Sergey Brin co-founded Google.

Before the internet became commonplace people relied on books and journals. People used to read encyclopaedias and visit libraries to get information. These days search engines provide easy access to information. Search engines have become faster over the years and the ability to index information has also increased tremendously. This has enabled us to search for and access information easily.

We can search by speaking to a phone. How does that work?

Smartphones have voice-controlled **virtual assistants** powered by search engines. Applications such as Siri, Alexa and Cortona are examples of digital virtual assistants. They convert the question asked verbally into text and use a search engine to find the results.

- The first popular search engine on the internet was Yahoo!
- Around the turn of the millennium, in the year 2000, Google's search engine rose to prominence.

3 steps of Search Engines: Crawling, Indexing and Ranking

Crawling

Indexing
Ranking

1 Unscramble these words related to a search engine.

a. RWGNILAC ____________

b. IDSEPR ____________

c. VCELERANE ____________

d. DXINE ____________

e. LKNEYPRHI ____________

f. ITULARV SISAATNST ____________

g. TEIEBWS ____________

h. EWB RESDASD ____________

i. EAPG NRKA ____________

j. RHSECA ____________

2 Explore the context of a search.

Open any search engine in your browser.

Search for the phrases 'bat', 'flying bat', 'wooden bat' and 'flying wooden bat'.

Did you notice that the search results differ based on the context of the search?

3 Use a search engine to answer the following trivia.

- Which was the first search engine?
- Which was the first website?
- Name five different search engines

4 HTML stands for Hypertext Markup Language. It allows you to create and structure sections, paragraphs, headings, images and links for web pages. Can you create an HTML page following these steps?

Open a text editor.

Type these lines into the text editor.

```
<!DOCTYPE html>
<html>
    <body>

        <h1>Welcome to my webpage</h1>
        <p>This is so much fun</p>

    </body>
</html>
```

Save this file as MyPage.html and open it in a browser.
Open MyPage.html and add these lines before the </body> tag.

```
    <br/>
    <br/>
    <a href=“https://www.radishtales.
    com/”>Radish Tales!</a>
```

```
<!DOCTYPE html>
<html>


     <body>
     <h1>Welcome to my webpage</h1>
     <p>This is so much fun</p>
     <br/>
     <br/>
     <a href="https://www.radishtales.
     com/">Radish Tales!</a>
     </body>


</html>
```

Open the page again in the browser and you can now see the link. Click on the link and the website will open in the browser.

Artificial Intelligence

INSIDE INTELLIGENT MACHINES!

**It is amazing what computers can do!
Are computers smarter than humans?**

Computers outperform humans in certain areas and humans outperform computers in other areas. Let us start by understanding the difference between humans and computers. The human brain helps us to think and act. We have emotions and feelings whereas computers do not have feelings and can consistently execute tasks without getting bored or tired.

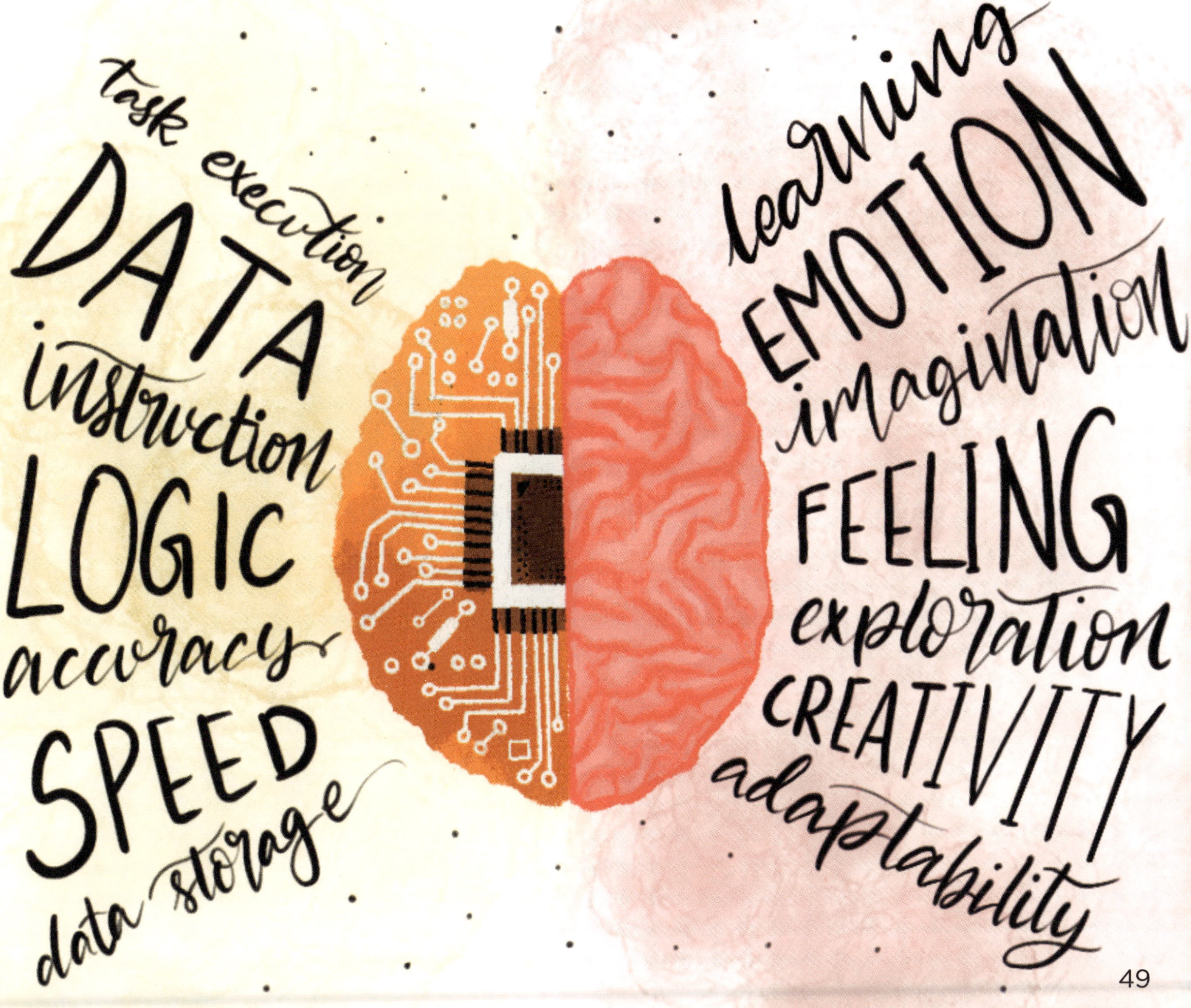

task execution
DATA
instruction
LOGIC
accuracy
SPEED
data storage
learning
EMOTION
imagination
FEELING
exploration
CREATIVITY
adaptability

Computers are programmed to execute instructions in a logical way. They cannot deviate from the programmed logic. Humans can deviate from typical logic based on the situation. For example, if the activity to be performed is to cross a street, a robot would simply cross the street whereas a human may also help an elderly person who is trying to get across. This is called **emotional thinking**.

Humans are capable of using imagination to solve a given problem in many different ways, whereas computers can solve the problem by following a set of instructions. Humans also try to explore the unknown and develop knowledge in areas where knowledge is limited. Humans are constantly developing new ideas.

Computers fare better than humans in data storage, speed and accuracy. Computers execute instructions whereas humans learn and adapt every day.

The power of computers is mind-boggling! Is there anything computers are not good at?

There are certain areas where humans have a far superior ability than computers. Let us take a step back and understand different ways of solving problems. Problem solving is of two types – **structured problem solving** and **unstructured problem solving**.

Structured problem solving

Unstructured problem solving

In structured problem solving, there are defined steps to solve a problem. Computers do well in structured problem solving where the computer or a system executes a defined set of instructions coded in a **software program**.

In unstructured problem solving, there are no defined steps to solve the problem and it often involves judgement, experience and intuition. Humans are good at unstructured problem solving. As technology evolves, computers are being programmed to deal with unstructured problems. As of now, humans are better at it. The field of computer science where computers exhibit certain human-like problem-solving abilities is called **Artificial Intelligence** or AI.

What is artificial intelligence?

Artificial intelligence is the ability of computers to perform tasks that require understanding and logic.

Can computers learn like humans?

Computers can learn, but their learning process is very different from that of humans. A child can easily differentiate between the pictures of a tiger and a leopard. A computer needs to be given rules that will help it to differentiate between a tiger and a leopard. This process is called **machine learning**. With machine learning, the computer can be trained using a large number of images of tigers and leopards to differentiate between them. The machine's learning ability improves as it is trained with more data.

Types of Artificial Intelligence

Artificial Narrow Intelligence

Artificial Narrow Intelligence (ANI) is exhibited by systems that can perform specific tasks on their own without human intervention. These systems flawlessly perform tasks that they have been programmed for. Artificial Narrow Intelligence is fairly commonplace today.

Artificial General Intelligence

Artificial General Intelligence (AGI) is the next level of artificial intelligence where systems can understand context and emotion. These systems can learn, perceive and operate like humans.

Artificial Super Intelligence

Artificial Super Intelligence (ASI) is the final stage of artificial intelligence where the system is aware of itself. At this point, the system will have the ability to think and will probably be superior to humans.

Is there a way to check if a computer can exhibit artificial intelligence?

Alan Turing, a famous English mathematician, came up with a test to check if a computer can think like a human. In this test, a human examiner has a conversation with unseen players. If a computer participates in this test and can trick the examiner into thinking it is a human being, it is said to pass the **Turing test**.

During the Turing test, a human questioner asks both respondents a series of questions. After a specified time, the questioner tries to decide which terminal is operated by a human respondent and which terminal is operated by a computer.

Is artificial intelligence commonplace? Do we use it in everyday life?

Artificial Narrow Intelligence is a form of artificial intelligence where a system is programmed to perform a single task intelligently like driving a car or playing chess. Each system is an expert in its respective area. For example, a self-driving artificial intelligence system can drive a car without human intervention.

The self-driving car can:

- slow down when the car encounters vehicles ahead,
- make turns in the correct places,
- drive within speed limits,
- avoid other vehicles and change lanes and
- use indicators and follow traffic rules.

Here are some more examples of Artificial Narrow Intelligence.

- Virtual assistants like Siri, Alexa, Cortana and Google Assistant
- Face-recognition technology
- Recommendation engines that suggest what to watch or buy based on past behaviour
- Go playing computers such as AlphaGo

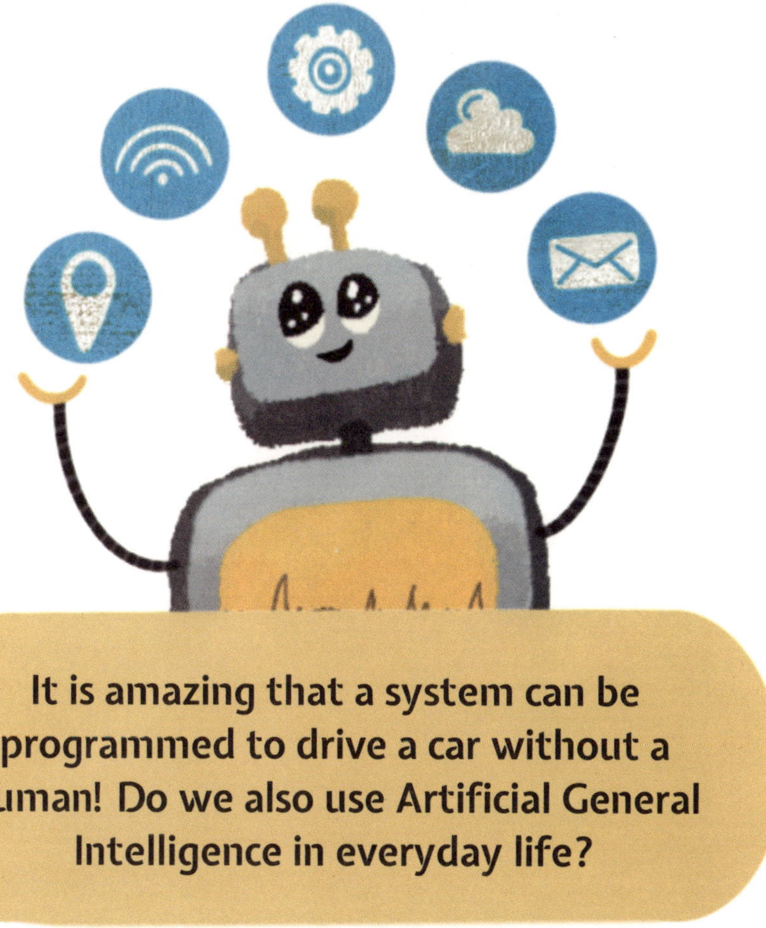

Artificial General Intelligence has not been achieved as of today. While a coffee-making robot that can prepare and serve coffee is an example of Artificial Narrow Intelligence, a robot that can enter any home and make coffee with the ingredients available in that home is an example of Artificial General Intelligence.

In Artificial Narrow Intelligence, the robot knows how to operate a specific type of coffee machine to brew coffee. In Artificial General Intelligence, the robot can brew coffee in any home with the ingredients and equipment available in that home. In this case, the robot needs to display situational awareness. It needs to go to the kitchen and look for coffee, sugar and milk. It needs to understand the type of coffee machine available and operate it to brew coffee. While this seems simple for a human, it is tough for a robot and that is why it is called Artificial General Intelligence.

It would be awesome if robots can behave like humans! I wonder who would win if computers play chess against humans.

There are artificial intelligence systems like DeepBlue that can play chess. Like chess, there is another strategy game called Go. An artificial intelligence system called AlphaGo plays Go very well and has defeated several human grandmasters.

It is important to understand however that we humans have general intelligence which means that we can play Go and also learn and do other things. The self-driving artificial intelligence system can only drive a car and cannot play Go or chess. This ability of humans to learn many different things is what sets them apart from current artificial intelligence systems which can do one thing very well. In the future, we may have artificial intelligence which can learn like humans and at that point, we would have successfully created Artificial General Intelligence.

The Three Laws of Robotics

In 1942, the science fiction writer Issac Asimov wrote the three laws of robotics to keep machines in check!

First Law

A robot may not injure a human being or, through inaction, allow a human being to come to harm.

Second Law

A robot must obey the orders given it by human beings except where such orders would conflict with the First Law.

Third Law

A robot must protect its own existence as long as such protection does not conflict with the First or Second Law.

1 Name two areas in which computers fare better than humans.

2 Name two areas in which humans fare better than computers.

3 Name two artificial intelligence systems that you have used.

4 Identify the type of artificial intelligence (ANI or AGI).

Self-driving car

Chess-playing program

A system enrolls in a university, takes the same classes that a human would and clears the exams.

A system enters a home and makes breakfast.

I
O
T

Internet of Things

SMART THINGS IN A SMART WORLD

I am amazed at the power of technology! The lights in my friend's home can be controlled remotely by an Application (App) on the phone!

The power of technology is amazing indeed! Remotely controlled 'smart' electrical appliances in your friend's home are examples of '**Internet of Things**' **or IoT**. The '**smart**' light is connected to the internet through the Wi-Fi network of your friend's home. An App on the smartphone is used to control the smart light.

Connected ecosystem

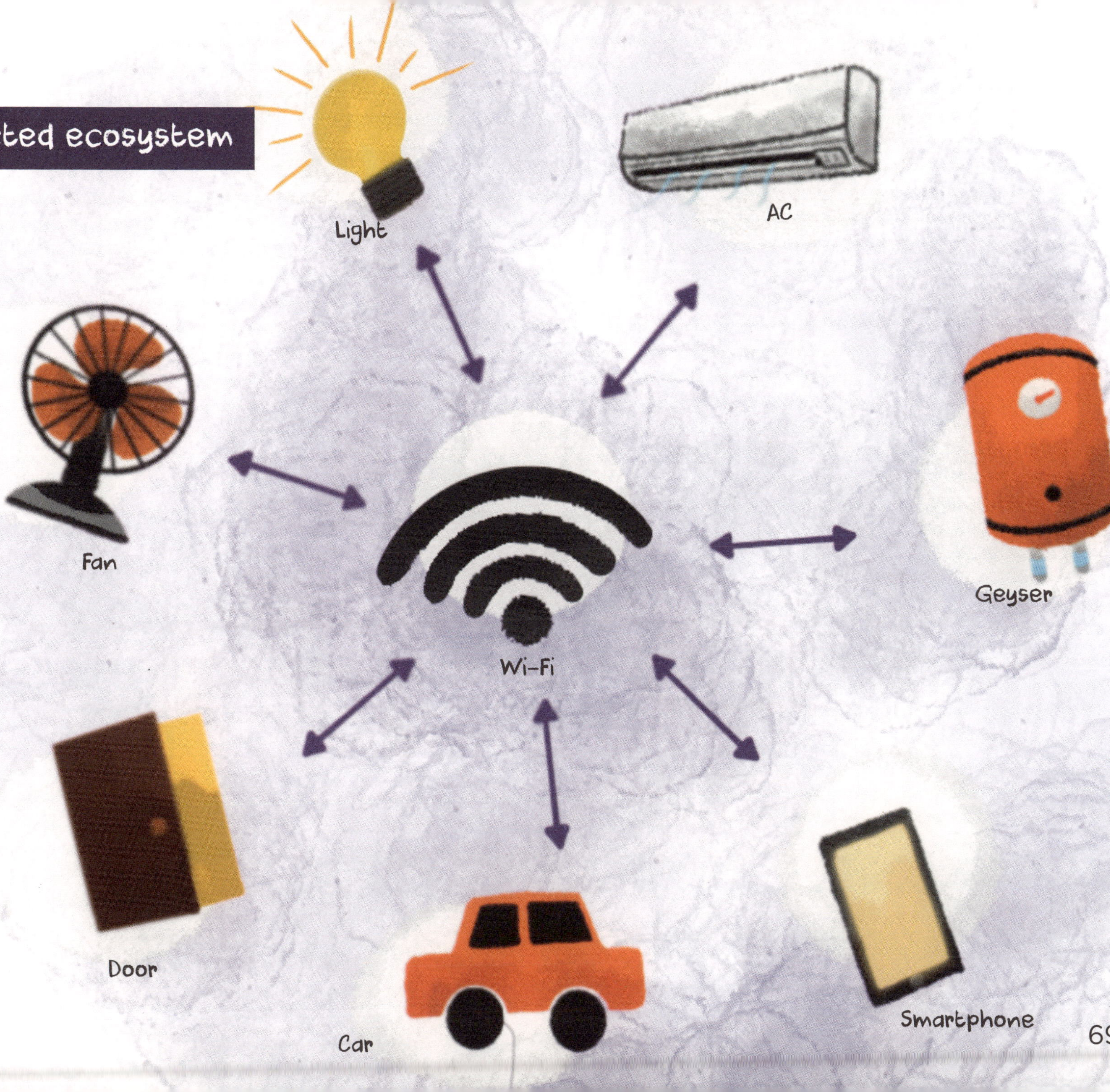

What is 'Internet of Things'? We learnt that the internet is a network of computers. Is this a different network?

The internet is a network of computers. IoT is a system in which devices equipped with electronic components, software and sensors are connected to each other and the internet. The smart light is a '**thing**' that is connected to the internet. In the absence of a working internet connection it can also connect to a smartphone via Bluetooth. Similarly, other 'things' such as refrigerators, air conditioners, water heaters and cars can also be connected to each other and the internet.

Does a smart light bulb behave like a computer?

A smart light bulb is an internet-capable device. It is built to perform a limited number of 'smart' actions such as changing the colour of the light, adjusting its brightness and switching on and off.

Can any device be connected to the internet?

The smart bulb has a small **embedded electronic chip** (also called an **integrated circuit**). We can add such chips to devices and enable them to connect to the internet. With IoT, different devices are connected to the internet enabling a 'smart' ecosystem that can make our lives easier by automating everyday activities.

Are there more examples of automation in everyday life?

Here are some examples of IoT that help automate human tasks.

SMART HOMES

A smart home uses devices connected to the internet that allow its residents to remotely manage and monitor their home. The data collected can also be used for various purposes such as efficient energy management and real-time security alerts.

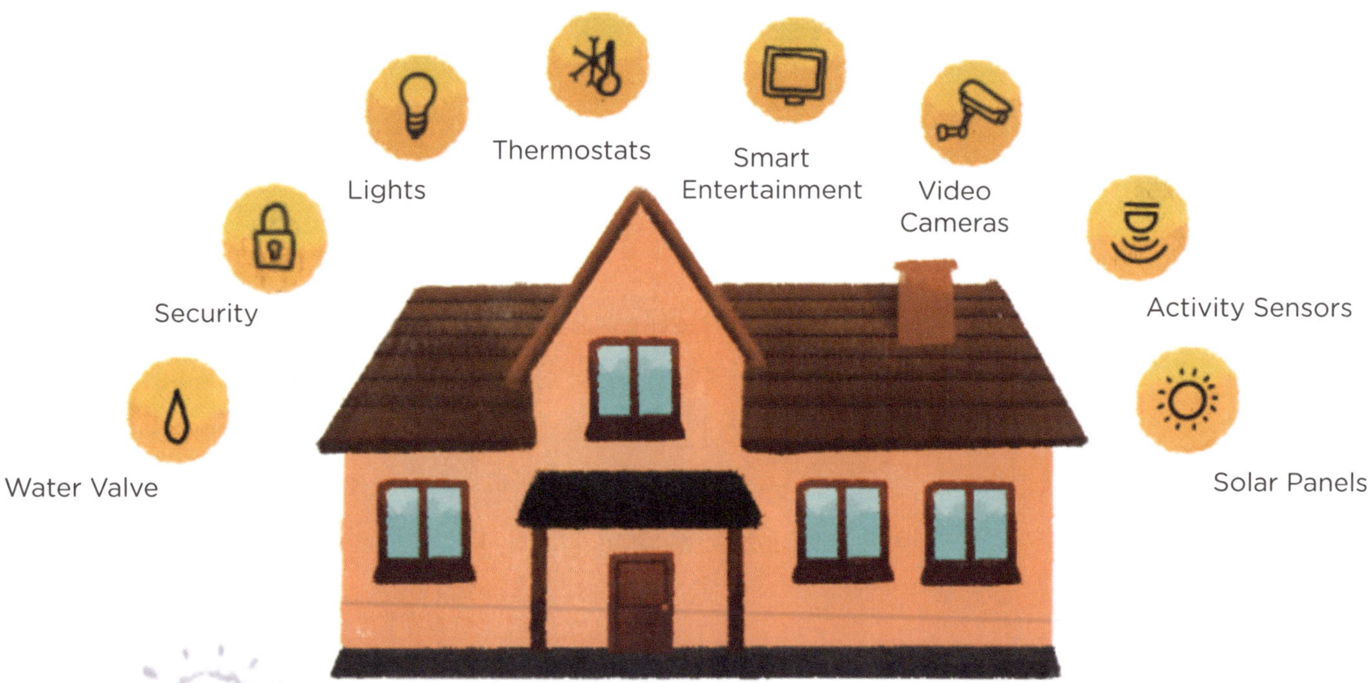

SMART TRAFFIC CONTROL SYSTEMS

Cameras installed on traffic intersections can capture traffic violations. The traffic control system can also record traffic and identify if an accident has occurred or if there is traffic congestion. Smart traffic control systems installed across a city can help manage traffic effectively.

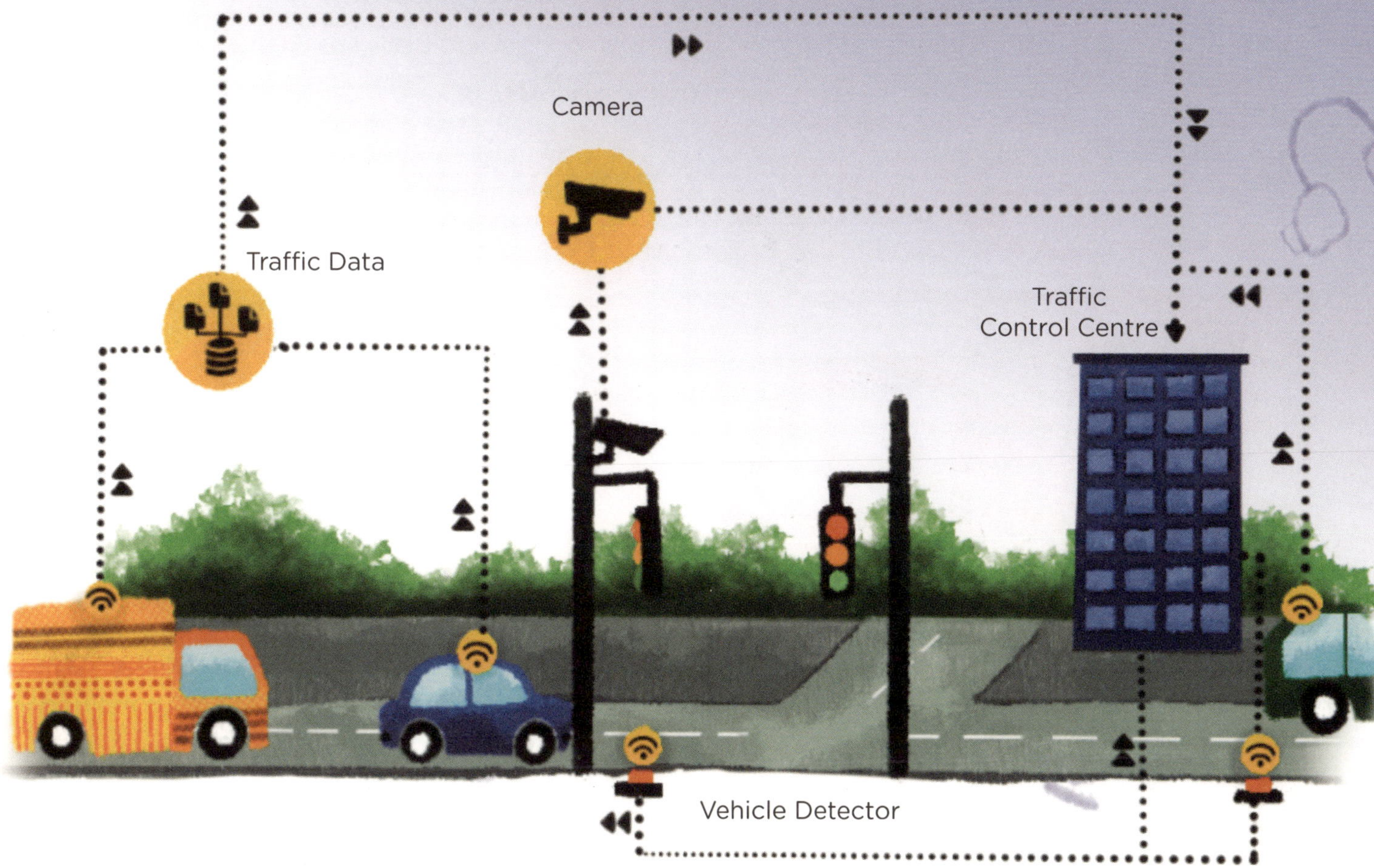

SMART TRUCKS

Smart trucks are connected, intelligent vehicles that interact with technology applications on the internet to improve safety and reduce wastage of goods.

Smart trucks have sensors to track various data points such as their location, speed, vehicle condition and temperature in the cargo carrier. This ensures that the truck is working effectively and the cargo is managed safely, reducing delays and wastage.

For example, certain medicines or food have to be maintained at a constant temperature. With smart trucks, the temperature of the cargo carrier can be adjusted based on external weather conditions.

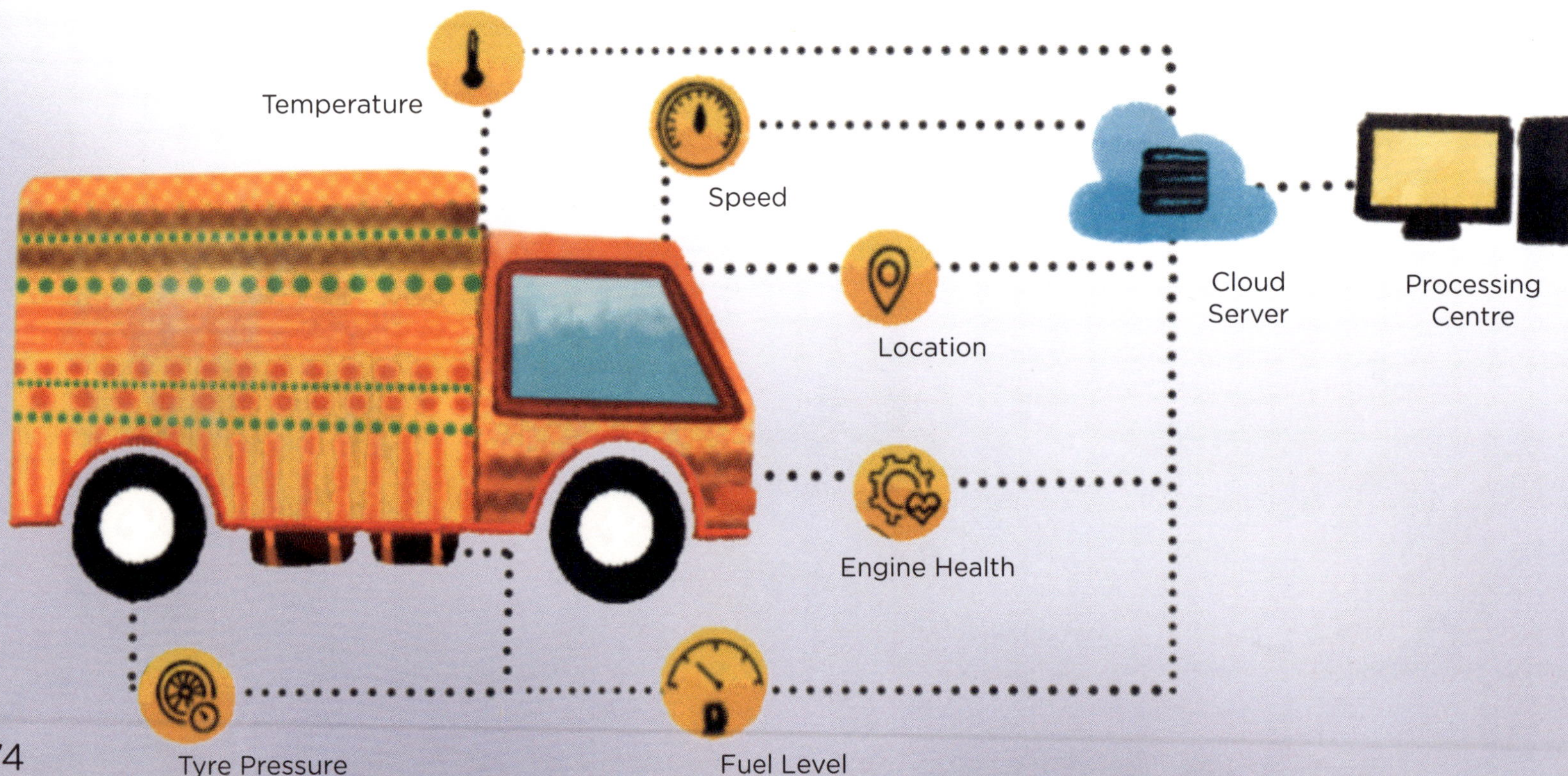

SMART CITIES

A smart city uses different types of sensors to collect data. Insights gained from the data are used to manage and improve operations across the city.

For example, a smart traffic control system can identify traffic congestion in an area. This data can be passed on to public transport systems to add more buses and run more intra-city trains.

Smart lighting can optimize energy usage by switching lights on automatically when it is dark and switching them off when there is sufficient light.

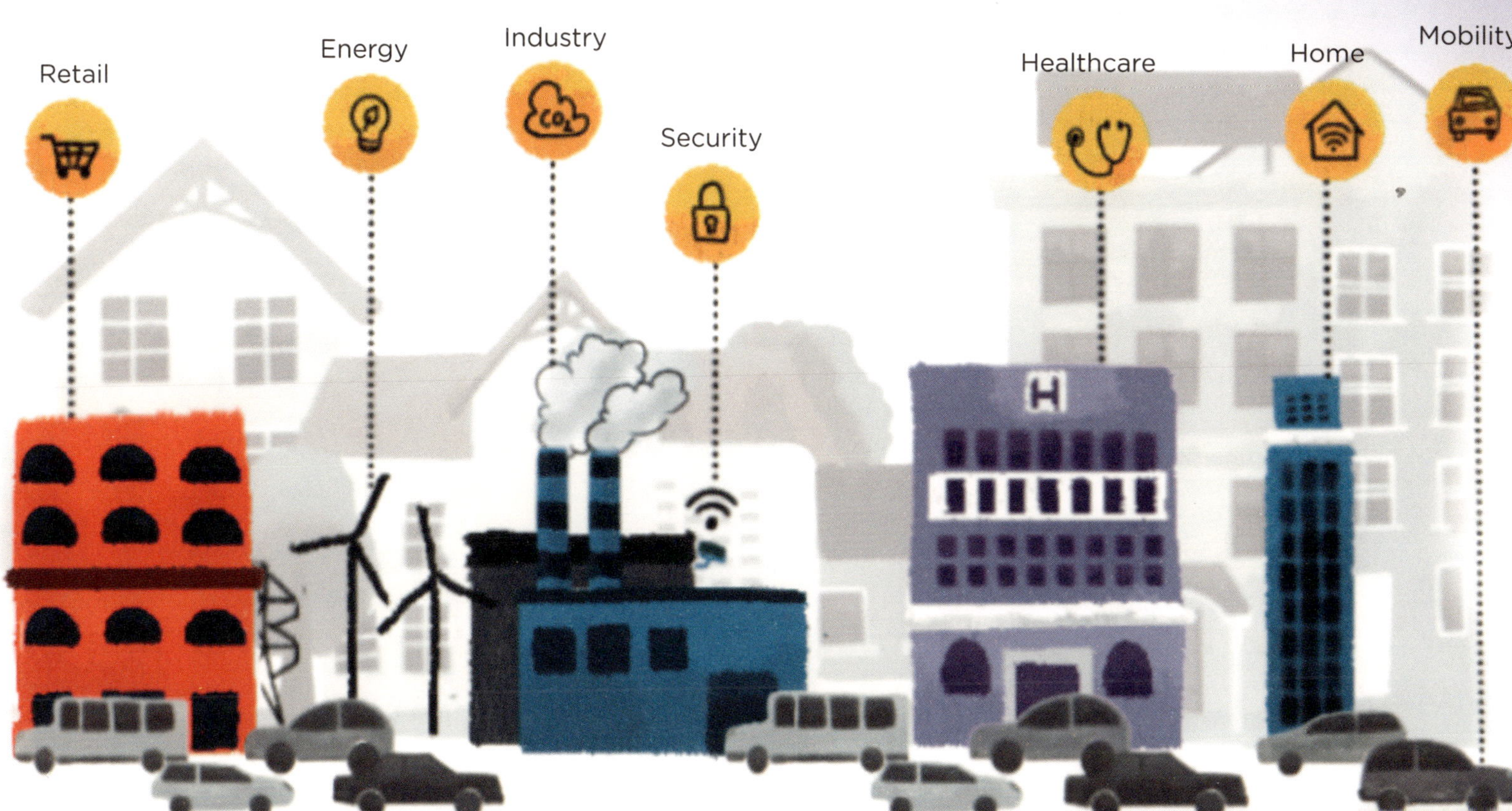

It is fascinating that so many devices can connect to the internet. How does IoT work?

The major components of IoT are Things, Connectivity, Cloud and Edge.

1. **Things**: 'Things' are devices and sensors which collect data. Some common sensors are:
   - Temperature sensors and thermostats
   - Pressure sensors
   - Humidity sensors
   - Light intensity detectors
   - Moisture sensors
   - Proximity detectors

2. **Connectivity**: 'Things' are connected to a public or private network. This is essential to transmit data to the central hub.

3 **Cloud**: 'Cloud' is the central hub where all collected data is processed and stored. Artificial intelligence systems process the data collected and perform appropriate actions.

4 **Edge**: These days, the 'connectivity' layer has become smart and can run artificial intelligence programs locally. This is called '**edge computing**' as the data is being processed at the edge of the cloud instead of in the cloud. This provides rapid turnaround time.

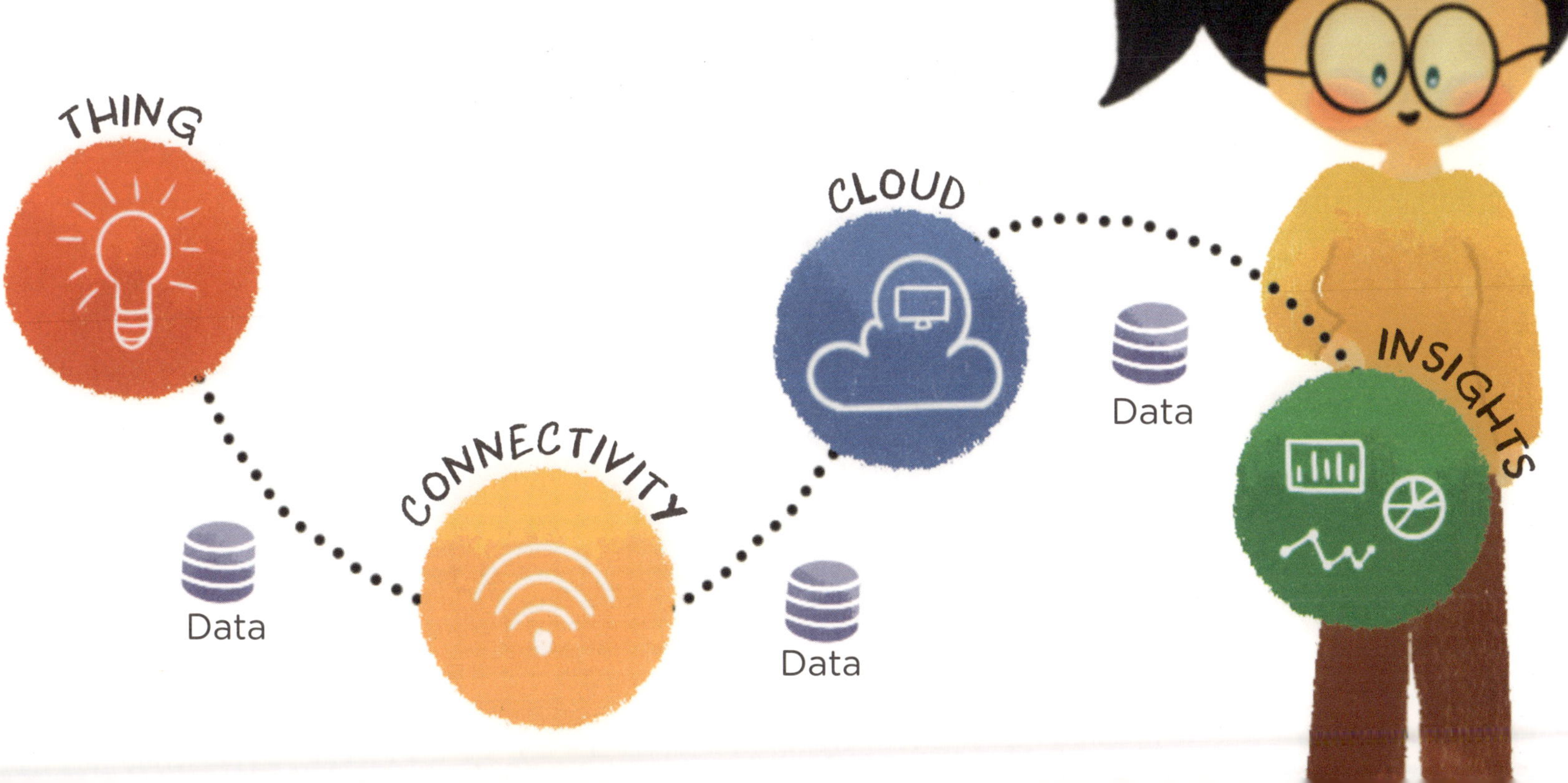

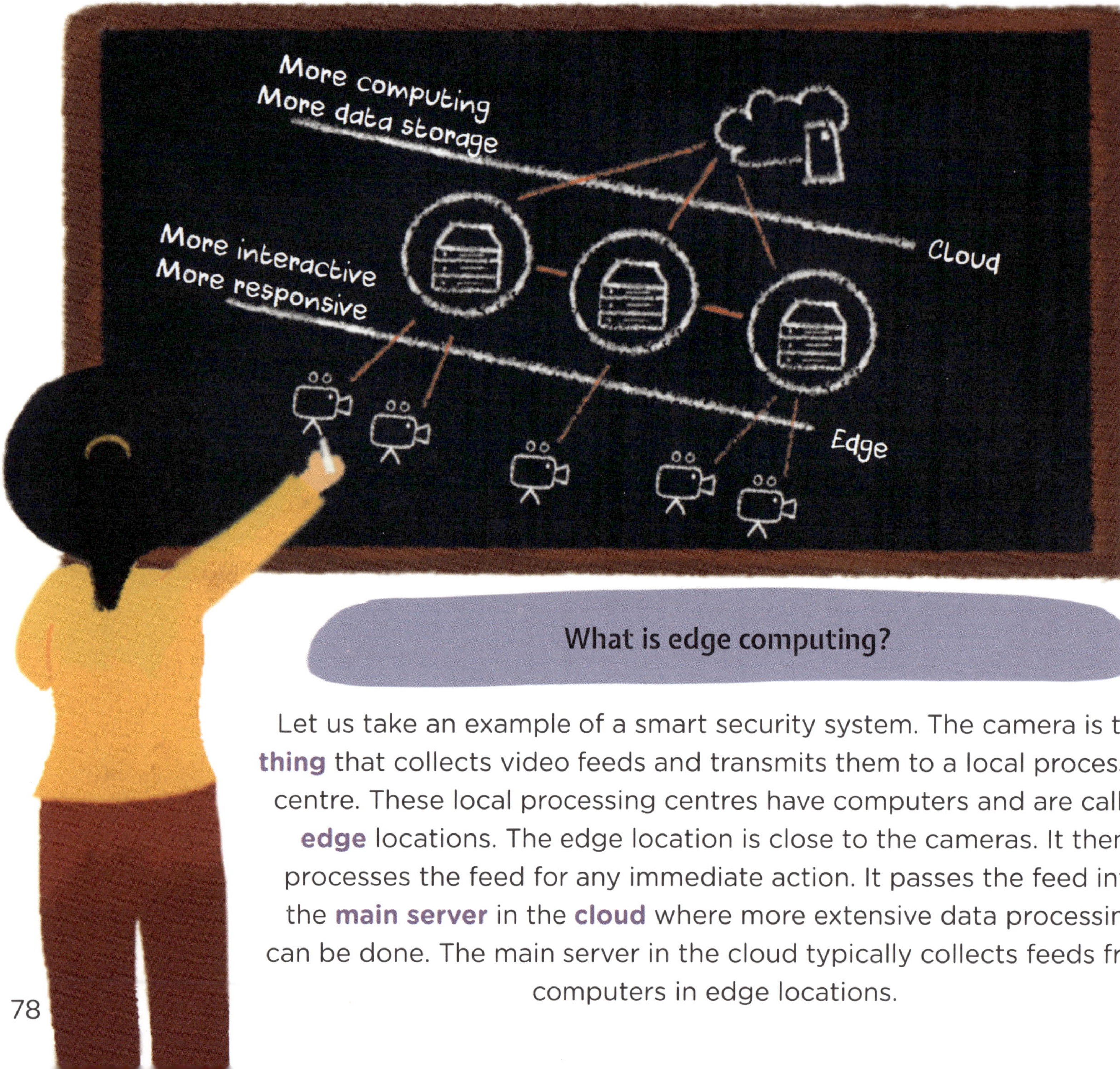

What is edge computing?

Let us take an example of a smart security system. The camera is the **thing** that collects video feeds and transmits them to a local processing centre. These local processing centres have computers and are called **edge** locations. The edge location is close to the cameras. It then processes the feed for any immediate action. It passes the feed into the **main server** in the **cloud** where more extensive data processing can be done. The main server in the cloud typically collects feeds from computers in edge locations.

1 Which of the following is not a component of IoT?

Smart bulb ☐

Newspaper ☐

Smartphone ☐

Temperature sensor ☐

2 A hotel is setting up an IoT network with sensors. Suggest ways in which the data generated by these sensors can be used.

Motion sensor

Smart key

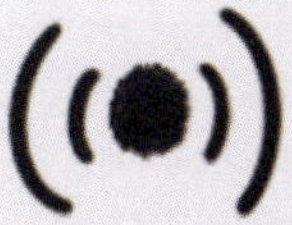

Air Conditioner sensor

Extended Reality

EXTENDING BEYOND THE REAL WORLD

There are games in which you can see animated characters as if they are present in our surroundings. How does that work?

Games in which the application (or App) adds **animations** to the players' surroundings are examples of **augmented reality**. The word 'augment' means to 'add something'. When real-world objects are enhanced with computer-generated virtual objects, it is called augmented reality. The App introduces the virtual characters into the real-world environment which which makes the player imagine that the characters actually exist. Augmented reality (AR) and **virtual reality (VR)** are types of **extended reality**.

The patent for the first VR headset was granted in 1960. The headset was named the 'Telesphere Mask' by inventor Morton Heilig.

What is extended reality?

Extended reality is the use of technology to create a simulated environment. With extended reality, one can interact with a digitally created three-dimensional (3D) environment by using devices like special headsets, controllers, goggles and gloves fitted with sensors. The device typically consists of a headset that covers the person's eyes and can either display a completely new surrounding with virtual reality or augment the person's environment with virtual objects through augmented reality. The headset has one screen for each eye and sensors to detect where the person is looking. The headset knows if the person is looking to the right, left, up or down. It then adjusts the image displayed on the screen accordingly so it looks real and natural.

Smartphones can double up as virtual reality devices. Simple VR headsets can be paired with smartphones to experience virtual reality.

How does extended reality work?

The human brain depends on sense organs such as the eyes, ears, nose and skin to perceive and experience the surroundings. The brain interprets information from the sense organs enabling humans to experience the environment around them. For example, the experience of a train approaching is created by the eyes seeing the train moving, the ears hearing the sound of the train and the body feeling vibrations when the train is close. Amongst the various sense organs, the brain relies primarily on vision. Each eye views the surroundings from a slightly different viewpoint. The brain merges the views from both eyes enabling **perception of depth**. The combination of all views processed by the brain enables humans to experience their surroundings. Extended reality headsets also mimic perception of depth, creating an illusion of being a part of the picture instead of looking at a picture .

Being a part of the picture

Looking at the picture

The Sensorama is one of the earliest known examples of virtual technology. It simulated a two-wheeler ride through New York City. In a prototype created by Morton Heilig in 1962, the user would experience a virtual ride through a screen. Fans were used to generate wind and special odour emitters were used to create smells of the city such as exhaust fumes and hot pizza.

A downside of extended reality is **cybersickness**. It is a feeling of nausea that can be caused by delays between the vision the brain expects and the image seen on the device. While using a virtual reality device, a person's eyes may perceive movement but the body remains still. There might also be a lag between the movement of a person's head and the screen adjusting to that movement. In such cases, the person may experience sickness. Extended reality technology is evolving to avoid cybersickness.

What is the difference between augmented reality and virtual reality?

Augmented reality is an interactive experience of the real world enhanced by adding virtual objects to our surroundings. For example, with augmented reality we can see dinosaurs around us.

Virtual reality is an interactive experience where the real world is replaced completely by virtual images and objects making us think that we are in a different place. For example, with virtual reality we can experience the illusion of being transported into the world of dinosaurs.

With augmented reality we can see dinosaurs around us.

With virtual reality we can experience the illusion of being transported into the world of dinosaurs.

What are the real-world uses of extended reality?

Here are a few applications of extended reality.

Gaming

Gaming is the most popular use of extended reality. Virtual reality can mimic or simulate the real world creating an illusion that the setting of the game is real.

Medical Training

Virtual reality can be used to train medical students for surgery in a controlled environment. This helps to mimic different scenarios for the student to work in without actually performing the surgery.

Military Training

Virtual reality is used to train soldiers and enables them to practise different battle scenarios.

Education

Virtual reality can also help to enhance learning. It can be used to see how the earth and moon look from space making learning experiential.

Immersion in video games is a psychological phenomenon where the player feels that they are a part of the world created by the game. Virtual reality is the next step for such games by transporting the players into a virtual world leading to full immersion.

1 Is this an example of virtual reality or augmented reality?

Walking on the moon

____

Flying over the Eiffel Tower

____

Seeing a tiger in your bedroom

____

Seeing a miniature Eiffel Tower in your room

____

2 Write down two practical uses for:

Virtual reality	Augmented reality
___________	___________
___________	___________

3 Seeing in stereo

This experiment shows that there is a slight difference between what your left eye and right eye see.

Step 1
Hold out a finger.

Step 2
Close your left eye and look at your finger with only your right eye.

Step 3
Then, close your right eye and look at your finger with only your left eye.

Cyber Safety

STAY SAFE WHILE YOU SURF!

We have got a glimpse into the power of technology and how it can transform our lives. The saying

great power comes with great responsibility

is applicable to the use of technology too. There are billions of users on the internet and not everyone has good intentions. We should be aware of bad actors and risks of online exposure. **Cyber safety** or e-safety is being safe while using the internet. We should be responsible users of the internet.

What should we be aware of while using the internet?

Information we share

The information or data that we leave on the internet is referred to as our **digital footprint.** We should be aware of our digital footprint as it remains on the internet forever.

People we e-meet

There are bad actors who try to lure and entrap people on the internet. We should be cautious while interacting with strangers who can potentially misuse our data.

Malicious websites

There are websites created with the intention of tricking internet users and stealing data. We should ensure that the websites we use are trusted and legitimate.

Digital etiquette

Digital etiquette refers to standards of conduct while using the internet. Similar to how we are expected to follow social etiquette during our social and personal interactions, we are expected to follow digital etiquette during our online interactions.

Tell me more about digital footprint.

Digital footprint refers to the trail of data left behind by internet users. This can be information that is voluntarily shared or data captured when we use the internet. There are internet users who have malicious intent and attempt to misuse data to their advantage. We need to be aware of our digital footprint and prevent unauthorized access to our data.

For example, when we use social media we should understand who has access to view our posts. Social media sites provide **privacy settings** that control how the data is handled. We should review and understand privacy settings to ensure that we control and protect our data.

How do we know if a website is safe to use?

We can do the following to check if a website is safe to use.

1. Ensure there is a lock symbol beside the website address. The lock indicates that the connection between the browser and the website is secure. A secure connection ensures that nobody can snoop on or modify data exchanged between the browser and the website.

2. Check the website name carefully as bad actors spoof popular websites to trick internet users into believing that the website is genuine.

Notice that the website displays the WhatBank logo but the website address is www.yyy.aa/whatbank which is suspicious.

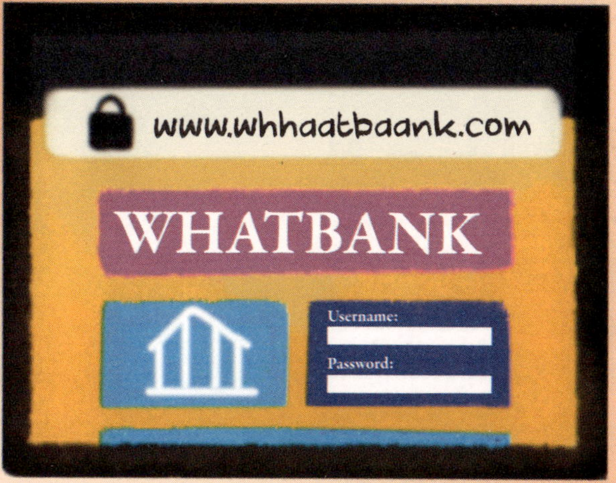

In this example, the website address www.whhaatbaank.com is a misspelling of the name 'WhatBank' which is also suspicious.

3

There are tools to check if a website can be trusted. Anti-virus software can scan websites we visit for **malware**.

How can people cheat us online?

Phishing and **Trojan Horses** are examples of how people can cheat us online. Technology is powerful and can help us in many ways. At the same time, we should be aware of the associated risks.

What is Phishing?

Phishing is when an imposter poses as a valid organization or a service provider and seeks sensitive data such as passwords or personal data. Phishing is a form of **social engineering**. In most cases, the attacker strategically manipulates human emotions to access **Personally Identifiable Information (PII)** such as name, address, parents' names, etc.

Any information when used alone or with other relevant data to identify an individual is called PII. For example, if an imposter has access to PII such as name, address or date of birth they can call the customer care of a telecom service provider and attempt to block the phone number of the person.

It is important to remember that we should not share PII with strangers.
Vishing is over-the-phone phishing that attempts to trick users into disclosing sensitive data over the phone.

What is a Trojan Horse?

A **Trojan Horse** is a type of malicious software that appears to be legitimate. It tricks users into willingly running the software and attempts to spy on the user, steal data or do something harmful. Trojan Horses are generally propagated by some form of trickery like asking the user to click on pop-ups or download email attachments. We should not download and install software that we are not familiar with.

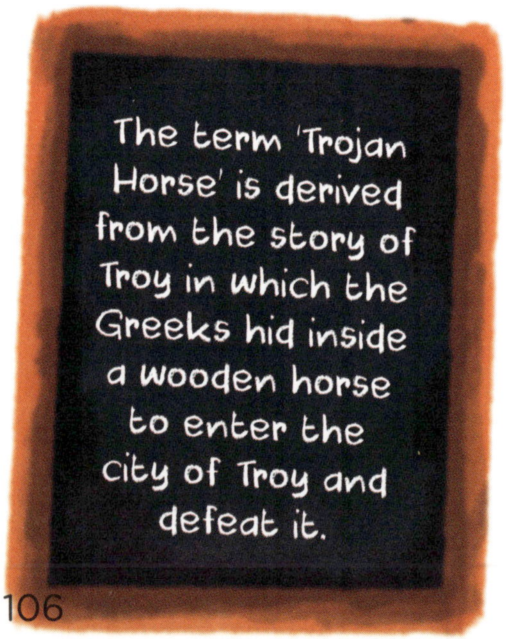

Are there guidelines to be aware of while posting data on the internet?

Here are some dos and don'ts to be aware of while posting data on the internet.

Don't share your passwords with others.

Don't share PII and whereabouts unless necessary.

Don't interact with strangers.

Don't share posts that your parents would not approve of.

Don't post when you are angry or upset.

Don't turn on location services unless necessary.

Don't meet online acquaintances in person without permission from your parents.

Remember to always follow digital etiquette.

What does digital etiquette mean?

Digital etiquette or **Netiquette** refers to standards of conduct while using the internet. It is similar to social behaviour and manners - be polite, respectful and assertive but not aggressive. When posting about others, we should ensure that we have their permission. Always remember the golden rule - 'Treat others as you would like to be treated.' Here are some tips on social media manners.

Don't bully or share hurtful comments or posts.

Don't tag or post photos of others without their permission.

Don't be impolite or use abusive language.

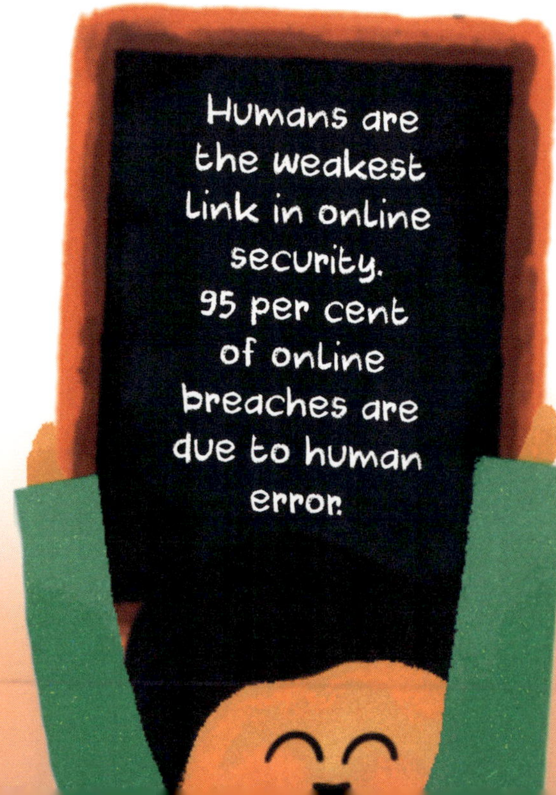

We should be careful about sharing personal information with strangers who could potentially misuse our data. We should be careful while interacting with strangers on the internet just the way we are careful with strangers in the real world. There are bad actors who can use certain websites to cheat and steal data. We should ensure that our parents are aware of the websites we use.

We should always use technology wisely and ethically. There are several websites that are immensely useful and only collect data required for the website to function. These reputed websites typically take stringent measures to protect the data of users.

1 You receive a call from someone you do not know. The person claims to be your parents' friend and asks for details like your parents' birth dates, their address, your grandparents' names and your pet's name. What should you do?

☐ Share the information.

☐ Don't share the information.

2 Can you list the features of a strong password?

should be eight characters or more

____

____

____

3 What does your digital footprint look like? Search the internet for your name and see if you have a digital footprint.

4 Which of the following is personally identifiable information?

- [ ] Your favourite colour
- [ ] Your home address
- [ ] Your favourite sport
- [ ] Your favourite movie

5 Search the internet about Clickbait and write down how you can avoid it.

Answers

Internet

1
- COMPUTER
- WORLD WIDE WEB
- MEGABIT
- SEA PLOUGH
- INTERNET
- WEBSITE
- REPEATER
- ROUTER
- PROTOCOL
- BROWSER

P	R	B	M	E	G	A	B	I	T	R	C	S
R	V	I	N	T	E	R	N	E	T	E	B	E
O	B	R	O	W	S	E	R	E	W	D	Y	A
T	N	C	L	C	A	W	N	S	O	N	T	P
O	S	O	R	E	W	E	B	S	I	T	E	L
C	B	M	R	O	S	E	G	N	U	O	F	O
O	P	P	S	E	U	S	I	L	T	E	R	U
L	O	U	L	E	P	T	P	Q	U	E	V	G
S	Z	T	P	E	R	E	E	N	E	C	L	H
Z	L	E	L	M	P	Q	U	R	G	E	B	U
W	O	R	L	D	W	I	D	E	W	E	B	R
O	W	Q	U	W	E	S	J	B	U	F	G	G
S	B	R	E	P	E	A	T	E	R	E	Y	E

Search Engine

1

a. CRAWLING
b. SPIDER
c. RELEVANCE
d. INDEX
e. HYPERLINK
f. VIRTUAL ASSISTANT
g. WEBSITE
h. WEB ADDRESS
i. PAGE RANK
j. SEARCH

Artificial Intelligence

1

a. Execution speed
b. Data storage

2

a. Emotional behaviour
b. Adaptable to change

4

Self-driving car - **ANI**
Chess-playing program - **ANI**
A system enrolls in a university, takes the same classes that a human would and clears the exams - **AGI**
A system enters a home and makes breakfast - **AGI**

Internet of Things

1 **Newspaper**
A newspaper is not an IoT component.

2 **Motion sensor**
Can be used to turn on the lights in a room when motion is detected

Smart key
Can be used to lock the door of the room if the person has left the room

Air Conditioner sensor
Can monitor wear and tear of the unit so that we can predict when it needs to be cleaned, etc.

Extended Reality

1 Walking on the moon - **Virtual reality**

Flying over the Eiffel Tower - **Virtual reality**

Seeing a tiger in your bedroom - **Augmented reality**

Seeing a miniature Eiffel Tower in your room - **Augmented reality**

2 **Virtual reality**
Education
Medical training

Augmented reality
Gaming
Military training

Cyber Safety

1 **Don't share the information**

You do not know the person and the questions are very generic. Such common questions are often used as security questions to secure accounts on the internet. By giving such information you may allow a stranger to impersonate your parents and access their phone number or bank accounts. This kind of attack is called **Vishing**.

2 a) should be eight characters or more

b) should have at least one number

c) should have at least one special character

d) should not be the same as your previous password

4 Your home address

Shalini Satish

Author

Shalini is a software engineer by profession and a writer by passion. She has over 15 years of experience in engineering and software development. She is a freelance writer and her work has been published in several local and national newspapers.

Raam Baranidharan

Author

Raam has over 15 years of experience in software platform development. Working with cutting-edge technologies has given him a ringside view of the latest developments in this field and the need for everyone to understand the impact of technology on their lives.

Disha Raam

Chief Curiosity Officer

Disha is the Chief Curiosity Officier of Radish Tales. Her curiosity to understand how things work and her constant questions were the motivation to create this book. Shalini and Raam along with their nine-year-old daughter Disha have founded Radish Tales to deliver educational content to young learners.

Nishi Banka

Illustrator

Nishi is a user experience designer, illustrator and visual communicator. She has a strong background in design and research. She has also been recognized as a 'Top Talent in Illustration' worldwide by Adobe. She loves to work on content for children and you can see more of her work on her instagram handle @nishi_creates.

Acknowledgements

This book would not have been possible without the support and encouragement of our family and friends.

We thank Veena Wadhwani for meticulously editing the content of the book.

We thank the team at HarperCollins for lending wings to our dream project.
Isha Nagar for her guidance on style and design.
Special thanks to Tina Narang for her constant support, guidance and patience. She has been the wind beneath the wings of this book.

... and the journey has just begun

The world of technology is vast and many 'advanced technologies' are making their way into our lives faster than we imagined. Young Techie Series (YTS) is a set of books about everyday technology for ages nine and up. Join Alia and Copa in the next book as they continue their journey exploring fascinating technologies.

Look out for more!